STUDY GUIDE

STANDING STRONG

IN THE

STORM

Copyright © 2022 by Greg Davis

Published by Arrows and Stones

All rights reserved. No portion of this book may be reproduced, stored in a retrieval system, or transmitted in any form or by any means—electronic, mechanical, photocopy, recording, scanning, or other—except for brief quotations in critical reviews or articles, without prior written permission of the author.

All Scripture quotations are taken from the Holy Bible, New International Version®, NIV®. Copyright © 1973, 1978, 1984, 2011 by Biblica, Inc.™ Used by permission of Zondervan. All rights reserved worldwide. www.zondervan.com. The "NIV" and "New International Version" are trademarks registered in the United States Patent and Trademark Office by Biblica, Inc.™

For foreign and subsidiary rights, contact the author.

Cover design by: Sara Young

Cover Photo by: Emily Shuff Photography

ISBN: 978-1-957369-92-1   1 2 3 4 5 6 7 8 9 10

Printed in the United States of America

STUDY GUIDE

STANDING STRONG
IN THE
STORM

ARROWS &
STONES

CONTENTS

Chapter 1. Wishing for a Nightmare 6

Chapter 2. It's Time to Cross Over 10

Chapter 3. Sent into the Storm 14

Chapter 4. Rough Seas: The Strength of the Storm 18

Chapter 5. Under His Feet 22

Chapter 6. The Inner Storm 26

Chapter 7. A Word from the Lord 30

Chapter 8. The Certainty of Uncertainty 34

Chapter 9. The Focus of Faith 38

Chapter 10. Rescue, Restoration, and Reflection 42

Chapter 11. When the Winds Die Down 46

Chapter 12. Partnering with God 50

Chapter 13. More Tips for the Tempest 54

Chapter 14. The Other Side:
             When You Have Crossed Over 58

I recommend Standing Strong in the Storm. This redemptive mixture of tough reality and triumphant faith is an important read for modern believers.
—DR. MARK RUTLAND

CULTIVATING RESILIENCE IN TIMES OF TROUBLE

STANDING STRONG IN THE STORM

GREG DAVIS

CHAPTER 1

WISHING FOR A NIGHTMARE

"We can get bitter, or we can get better. Nothing good ever comes from choosing the former."

READING TIME

As you read Chapter 1: "Wishing for a Nightmare" in Standing Strong in the Storm, reflect on the questions and scriptures.

REFLECT AND TAKE ACTION:

When have you questioned why God didn't intervene in a difficult situation? What happened?

_____
_____
_____
_____
_____
_____

Is there anything going on right now that you can't see God's reasoning in? What is it?

_____
_____
_____
_____
_____
_____

Why do you think sometimes God doesn't intervene? What do you think He wants us to do in those situations?

_____
_____
_____
_____
_____
_____

> *I will give thanks to you, LORD, with all my heart; I will tell of all your wonderful deeds. I will be glad and rejoice in you; I will sing the praises of your name, O Most High.*
>
> —*Psalm 9:1-2*

Consider the scripture above and answer the following questions:

How do you give thanks to God for the good He does as David did in this psalm?

_____
_____
_____
_____
_____

Do you ever have trouble praising God in the middle of troubling times?

_____
_____
_____
_____
_____

When was the last time you told others of the "wonderful deeds" of God?

_____
_____
_____
_____
_____

What has been a difficult situation that you've had to endure with God's help?

_____
_____
_____
_____

What questions, if any, did you have for God when the above occurred? Do you now have answers to these questions?

_____
_____
_____
_____
_____

How did your life's storm affect your faith? Was it affected positively or negatively?

_____
_____
_____
_____
_____

Despite being afraid or uncertain in this situation, did you strive to continue moving forward? What helped you or prevented you from moving forward?

_____
_____
_____
_____

CHAPTER 2

IT'S TIME TO CROSS OVER

"If you respond correctly to your storm, God can transform the pain of misery into the power of ministry."

READING TIME

As you read Chapter 2: "It's Time to Cross Over" in Standing Strong in the Storm, reflect on the questions and scriptures.

REFLECT AND TAKE ACTION:

Is there something God is calling you to do that you're hesitant to pursue? If so, what is it?

_____
_____
_____
_____
_____
_____

What do you feel is your life purpose? How has God used past events to prepare you for this purpose?

_____
_____
_____
_____
_____
_____

Is there anything you've conquered with the Lord's help that you thought you could never overcome?

_____
_____
_____
_____
_____
_____

> *And we know that in all things God works for the good of those who love him, who have been called according to his purpose. For those God foreknew he also predestined to be conformed to the image of his Son, that he might be the firstborn among many brothers and sisters.*
>
> —Romans 8:28-29

Consider the scripture above and answer the following questions:

What does the above verse mean when it speaks of those "who have been called according to his purpose"?

_____

_____

_____

_____

What does it mean to be conformed to the image of [God's] Son? Are you conformed to the image of Jesus Christ?

_____

_____

_____

_____

Do you think God uses the events in our life to help conform us to the shape of His son? What events has He used in your life?

_____

_____

_____

_____

_____

What do you feel are some of your current life barriers that you need to remove in order to cross over?

_____
_____
_____
_____
_____

Why do you think God is pushing you into this next season? Why can't you stay *where* you are and *who* you are?

_____
_____
_____
_____
_____

What next step is God prompting you to take? Can you see the full path in front of you or only the next step?

_____
_____
_____
_____
_____

What does your daily time with God look like? Where can you make improvements to get closer to Him?

_____
_____
_____
_____
_____

CHAPTER 3

SENT INTO THE STORM

"Not all storms in life are the result of disobedience. Sometimes, following God's will can take us right into the pathway of adversity."

READING TIME

As you read Chapter 3: "Sent into the Storm" in Standing Strong in the Storm, reflect on the questions and scriptures.

REFLECT AND TAKE ACTION:

Describe a storm that has occurred in your life. What have you learned or are you learning through this time?

_____
_____
_____
_____
_____
_____
_____

Do you ever question if storms are the best way we can learn? Why do you think God doesn't just give us the wisdom?

_____
_____
_____
_____
_____
_____
_____

How can the storms we experience help not only us but others?

_____
_____
_____
_____
_____
_____

> *Then King Nebuchadnezzar leaped to his feet in amazement and asked his advisers, "Weren't there three men that we tied up and threw into the fire?" They replied, "Certainly, Your Majesty." He said, "Look! I see four men walking around in the fire, unbound and unharmed, and the fourth looks like a son of the gods." Nebuchadnezzar then approached the opening of the blazing furnace and shouted, "Shadrach, Meshach and Abednego, servants of the Most High God, come out! Come here!" So Shadrach, Meshach and Abednego came out of the fire. . . .*
>
> —*Daniel 3:24-26*

Consider the scripture above and answer the following questions:

Why were Shadrach, Meshach, and Abednego punished for staying obedient and faithful to God?

_____
_____
_____
_____

Have you ever felt you encountered an adverse situation for obeying the Lord? What happened?

_____
_____
_____
_____

Other than God protecting Shadrach, Meshach, and Abednego, what good came from their situation?

_____
_____
_____
_____

Other than the storm you described in chapter 1 of this study guide, what other storms in life have you experienced? Have any of them been easier than others?

___

Was there a recurring struggle present among all of the storms you listed and described? How can you overcome this particular struggle?

___

In the midst of any of your storms, have you ever experienced a peace so great it must have been sent from God? When did you experience this, and what did it feel like?

___

Do you feel the above peace is always accessible to us? Why or why not?

___

CHAPTER 4

ROUGH SEAS: THE STRENGTH OF THE STORM

"It is not just important to overcome resistance. We need to overcome resistance the right way."

READING TIME

As you read Chapter 4: "Rough Seas: The Strength of the Storm" in *Standing Strong in the Storm*, reflect on the questions and scriptures.

REFLECT AND TAKE ACTION:

On whom do you tend to rely more—yourself or God—in the midst of adversity?

_____
_____
_____
_____
_____
_____
_____

What do you think the "right way" to overcome the storm is?

_____
_____
_____
_____
_____
_____
_____

Have you ever tried to overcome an adverse situation in a way that didn't work out or was the wrong way? What happened?

_____
_____
_____
_____
_____
_____

> *God is our refuge and strength, An ever-present help in trouble. Therefore we will not fear, though the earth give way and the mountains fall into the heart of the sea, though its waters roar and foam and the mountains quake with their surging.*
>
> —Psalm 46:1-3

Consider the scripture above and answer the following questions:

When in "trouble" like the verse mentions, what is your initial response?

_____
_____
_____
_____
_____

In your own words, what does it mean that God is your refuge? How do you live differently knowing this?

_____
_____
_____
_____
_____

Do you live with any fear present in your life? What is the fear tied to?

_____
_____
_____
_____
_____

How do you think you will respond in the face of adversity if you move forward *expecting* resistance?

_____

_____

_____

_____

How has God increased your spiritual strength or knowledge through your past life storms?

_____

_____

_____

_____

Did you recognize at the time this was what God was trying to accomplish? When did you discover it?

_____

_____

_____

_____

Whom do you look up to? If appropriate, contact them and ask for their advice on navigating difficult times. Write what they say below.

_____

_____

_____

_____

CHAPTER 5

UNDER HIS FEET

"As a child of God, there is nothing in our lives that Jesus can't defeat!"

READING TIME

As you read Chapter 5: "Under His Feet" in *Standing Strong in the Storm*, reflect on the questions and scriptures.

REFLECT AND TAKE ACTION:

Is Jesus the Lord over your entire life or just some areas? What areas of your life do you need to further submit to Him?

_____
_____
_____
_____
_____
_____
_____
_____
_____
_____

Do you think God's intervention in our troubles and storms is dependent on our obedience and submission to Him? Why or why not?

_____
_____
_____
_____
_____
_____
_____
_____
_____

> *And God placed all things under his feet and appointed him to be head over everything for the church, which is his body, the fullness of him who fills everything in every way.*
>
> *—Ephesians 1:22-23*

Consider the scripture above and answer the following questions:

What do you think this verse means when it says, "God placed all things under his feet"?

_____
_____
_____
_____
_____

Do you live your life like Jesus has it under His feet? In what areas are you not living like this is a reality?

_____
_____
_____
_____
_____

Is there anything you struggle to believe that God has complete control of? If yes, what is it?

_____
_____
_____
_____
_____

When, in the middle of your storm, has God shown you He had full authority over everything occurring? Describe the experience.

_____
_____
_____
_____

Rehash your list of difficult experiences you've been through that you made in chapter 3. What do you think was the enemy's goal in each of these situations?

_____
_____
_____
_____

What is one important lesson God has taught you in the midst of your life's storms? Do you think you could have learned this without the storm?

_____
_____
_____
_____

CHAPTER 6

THE INNER STORM

"We must not ever allow the enemy to build a stronghold in our lives because if we do, major warfare will be required for us to gain our freedom."

READING TIME

As you read Chapter 6: "The Inner Storm" in *Standing Strong in the Storm*, reflect on the questions and scriptures.

REFLECT AND TAKE ACTION:

Describe an area where a stronghold of the enemy could exist in your thinking.

_____
_____
_____
_____
_____
_____

What strongholds of thinking from the enemy have you worked to overcome with the Lord's help?

_____
_____
_____
_____
_____
_____

What mindsets or beliefs might you harbor in your thinking that could be coming from the enemy? How can you identify and rid yourself of these?

_____
_____
_____
_____
_____
_____

> *Why, LORD, do you stand far off? Why do you hide yourself in times of trouble?*
>
> —*Psalm 10:1*

Consider the scripture above and answer the following questions:

Have you ever felt God has stood far off during your time of trouble? Why do you think this happens?

_____
_____
_____
_____
_____

How do you respond to this feeling? How do you think God wants us to respond to this feeling?

_____
_____
_____
_____
_____

Do you think what we think and how we think it is important when trying to overcome storms in our life? Why or why not?

_____
_____
_____
_____
_____
_____

What negative ways of thinking have you had to discover and uproot to get your thinking right in the midst of a storm?

_____
_____
_____
_____

What are some new, positive ways of thinking you have adopted as you've learned from the storms God has brought you through in life?

_____
_____
_____
_____

Of all the principles and strategies discussed in this chapter, which can you and do you need to apply more effectively? List the ones you need to work on and how you can work on them each day.

_____
_____
_____
_____

CHAPTER 7

A WORD FROM THE LORD

"I can tell you from personal experience that if there's anything you are going to need in a time of storm, it is a word from the Lord."

READING TIME

As you read Chapter 7: "A Word from the Lord" in Standing Strong in the Storm, *reflect on the questions and scriptures.*

REFLECT AND TAKE ACTION:

Describe a time God has given you a word or a revelation from His Word that has helped you through a difficult time.

_____
_____
_____
_____
_____
_____

Is God's Word or going to God in prayer your first response to adverse situations? Why or why not?

_____
_____
_____
_____
_____
_____

Do you think God will ever not have a word for your situation or want you to find it out on your own? Why?

_____
_____
_____
_____
_____
_____

> *Your word is a lamp for my feet, a light on my path.*
>
> —Psalm 119:105

Consider the scripture above and answer the following questions:

What do you feel the meaning of this verse is? What does it look like when you live as if God's Word is a lamp for your feet and a light on your path?

_____
_____
_____
_____
_____

What occurs when we don't apply God's Word to our lives?

_____
_____
_____
_____

Has God's Word or a word from God ever guided you through a troubling and confusing time? Describe the situation.

_____
_____
_____
_____
_____
_____

How does spending daily time in God's Word prepare us for coming storms?

When have you or someone you know gotten a word from the Lord that wasn't from His Word but lined up with it? Describe the situation.

How did the above word impact and change your life?

What practical steps can you suggest to someone wanting to improve their daily devotional life and spend more time in God's Word?

CHAPTER 8

THE CERTAINTY OF UNCERTAINTY

"As we follow the example of Christ in the toughest days of our lives, we need to allow the certainty of our commitment to obey God's will to override any uncertainty regarding the details of God's plan."

READING TIME

As you read Chapter 8: "The Certainty of Uncertainty" in Standing Strong in the Storm, *reflect on the questions and scriptures.*

REFLECT AND TAKE ACTION:

Is there anything you are uncertain about in your walk with the Lord? If so, what is it?

_____
_____
_____
_____
_____
_____
_____

How can uncertainty damage one's relationship with God?

_____
_____
_____
_____
_____
_____
_____

Are uncertainty and doubt the same thing? In your own words, what is the difference?

_____
_____
_____
_____
_____
_____

> *Then Jesus went with his disciples to a place called Gethsemane, and he said to them, "Sit here while I go over there and pray." He took Peter and the two sons of Zebedee along with him, and he began to be sorrowful and troubled. Then he said to them, "My soul is overwhelmed with sorrow to the point of death. Stay here and keep watch with me."*
>
> —Matthew 26:36-38

Consider the scripture above and answer the following questions:

What example do you think Jesus was setting for us here?

_____
_____
_____
_____

What role does prayer play when you are faced with overwhelming sorrow or uncertainty?

_____
_____
_____
_____

Describe a storm in your life that led to newfound uncertainty.

_____
_____
_____
_____

Have you overcome the above uncertainty? What helped you conquer it?

_____
_____
_____
_____
_____

Do you have an inner circle? Who is a part of this inner circle?

_____
_____
_____
_____
_____

Besides God, whom do you trust more than anyone else?

_____
_____
_____
_____
_____

CHAPTER 9

THE FOCUS OF FAITH

"Our focus either empowers our faith or empowers our fear!"

READING TIME

As you read Chapter 9: "The Focus of Faith" in *Standing Strong in the Storm*, reflect on the questions and scriptures.

REFLECT AND TAKE ACTION:

Do you think faith is possible without focus? Why or why not?

_____
_____
_____
_____
_____
_____
_____

What are some things besides God that people put their faith in? What does that look like?

_____
_____
_____
_____
_____
_____
_____

How could a person's faith in God be strengthened?

_____
_____
_____
_____
_____
_____
_____

> *Everyone has heard about your obedience, so I rejoice because of you; but I want you to be wise about what is good, and innocent about what is evil. The God of peace will soon crush Satan under your feet.*
>
> —Romans 16:19-20

Consider the scripture above and answer the following questions:

Of all of God's names and titles, why do you feel Paul used "the God of peace" here?

___

___

___

___

___

What is the significance of Paul saying God will crush Satan under "your" feet instead of His own?

___

___

___

___

___

How can a person's fear be empowered by their focus? Describe that kind of experience.

___

___

___

___

___

When has your faith been empowered by your focus? What was the lesson you learned?

What commands from the Lord has fear hindered you from following?

Do you think the Lord recognizes the fear you have? What do you think He wants you to focus on instead? What would that look like?

CHAPTER 10

RESCUE, RESTORATION, AND REFLECTION

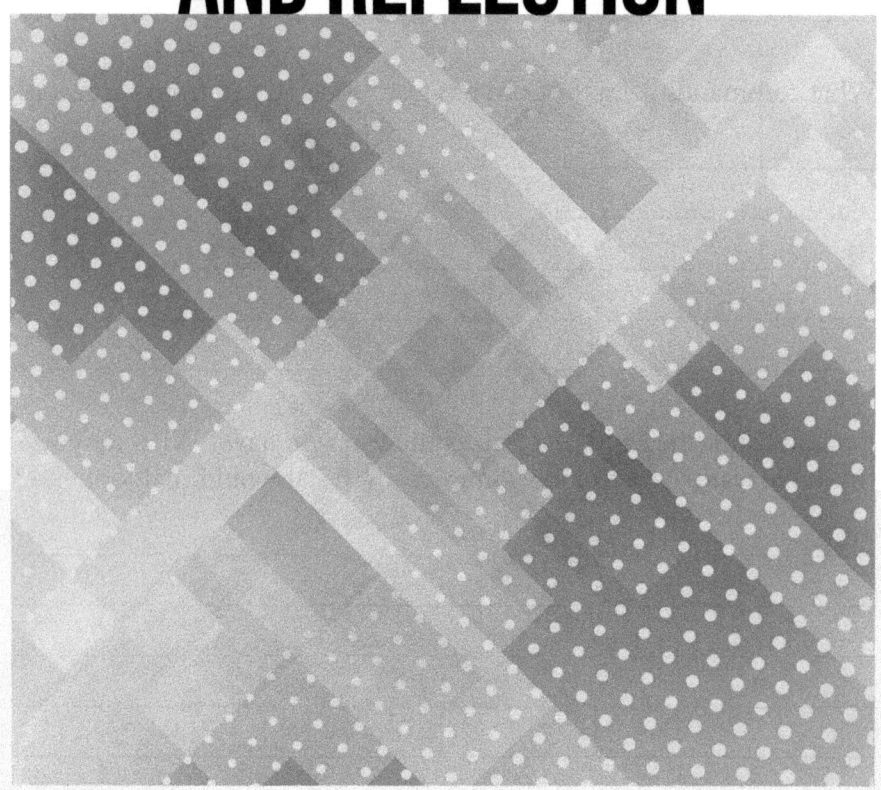

"Our thoughts are like an engine that pulls our emotions down the tracks. Where our thoughts go, our feelings follow."

READING TIME

As you read Chapter 10: "Rescue, Restoration, and Reflection" in *Standing Strong in the Storm*, reflect on the questions and scriptures.

REFLECT AND TAKE ACTION:

From what has God rescued you?

_____
_____
_____
_____
_____
_____
_____

How did God restore you after rescuing you from the above situation?

_____
_____
_____
_____
_____
_____
_____

What did you learn or discover about yourself and God through that experience?

_____
_____
_____
_____
_____
_____
_____

> *The weapons we fight with are not the weapons of the world. On the contrary, they have divine power to demolish strongholds. We demolish arguments and every pretension that sets itself up against the knowledge of God, and we take captive every thought to make it obedient to Christ.*
>
> —*2 Corinthians 10:4-5*

Consider the scripture above and answer the following questions:

What are the weapons that Paul writes about?

_____
_____
_____
_____
_____

What does Paul mean when he talks about strongholds? Where can we find these strongholds?

_____
_____
_____
_____
_____

Do you ever struggle to take your thoughts captive? What happens when people let fear, uncertainty, and doubt fester?

_____
_____
_____
_____
_____

How has the enemy succeeded in using distractions to turn you away from God's will for your life? What happened?

_____

_____

_____

_____

What strategies discussed in this chapter can you utilize to defend against the distractions of the enemy and get back on track to God's will?

_____

_____

_____

_____

_____

Which do you tend to focus on more: the failures in your life or the victories?

_____

_____

_____

_____

_____

What areas of your life do you need to reevaluate and reconsider according to the principles discussed in this chapter?

_____

_____

_____

_____

CHAPTER 11

WHEN THE WINDS DIE DOWN

"Trying to identify God's purpose can be a challenge while the storm continues to rage. But when the winds die down, we seem to be able to see more clearly."

READING TIME

As you read Chapter 11: "When the Winds Die Down" in *Standing Strong in the Storm*, reflect on the questions and scriptures.

REFLECT AND TAKE ACTION:

Have you ever been in a storm where you didn't understand God's plan until making it to the other side? Describe the experience.

_____
_____
_____
_____
_____
_____
_____
_____
_____
_____

Do you think sometimes God doesn't reveal His full plan so that we trust in Him more? Explain your answer.

_____
_____
_____
_____
_____
_____
_____
_____
_____
_____

> *And when they climbed into the boat, the wind died down. Then those who were in the boat worshiped him, saying, "Truly you are the Son of God."*
>
> —*Matthew 14:32-33*

Consider the scripture above and answer the following questions:

Why did the disciples only say Jesus was the Son of God after the winds had died down?

_____
_____
_____
_____
_____

Have you ever struggled to recognize God in the middle of your storm?

_____
_____
_____
_____
_____

When have you ever experienced the instruction, obstruction, and construction pattern occur in your life? What happened at each stage?

_____
_____
_____
_____
_____

What do you think God is calling you to accomplish with your life?

_____
_____
_____
_____
_____

In what areas are you aggressively and passionately pursuing God's calling on your life? In what areas are you not?

_____
_____
_____
_____
_____

What changes do you need to make to fully pursue God's plan for your life?

_____
_____
_____
_____
_____

CHAPTER 12

PARTNERING WITH GOD

"God will use your life in greater ways than you could ever imagine—IF you are willing to submit to His will and obey His Word."

READING TIME

As you read Chapter 12: "Partnering with God" in *Standing Strong in the Storm*, reflect on the questions and scriptures.

REFLECT AND TAKE ACTION:

Why do you think God wants to partner with people instead of just doing everything Himself?

_____
_____
_____
_____
_____
_____
_____
_____
_____
_____

What do you feel God wants to partner with you to accomplish through you? What's holding you back?

_____
_____
_____
_____
_____
_____
_____
_____
_____
_____

> *Praise be to the God and Father of our Lord Jesus Christ, the Father of compassion and the God of all comfort, who comforts us in all our troubles, so that we can comfort those in any trouble with the comfort we ourselves receive from God.*
>
> *—2 Corinthians 1:3-4*

Consider the scripture above and answer the following questions:

How do you share the comfort you receive from the Lord with others? When was the last time you did this? What was the result?

_____
_____
_____
_____
_____

Do you think the comfort of God is truly present in "all our troubles" as the verse states—or only some?

_____
_____
_____
_____
_____

When have you ever desired for God to completely intervene and better your situation without you having to put in any work? Why is this an incorrect way of thinking?

_____
_____
_____
_____

When have you partnered with God? What were you able to accomplish with His help?

_____
_____
_____
_____

Do you think your partnership with God is only for your benefit? Who else can benefit from it?

_____
_____
_____
_____

Have you ever taken a spiritual gifts assessment test? What are your spiritual gifts?

_____
_____
_____
_____

Take time to take or retake an assessment with either C. Peter Wagner's "Discover Your Spiritual Gifts" test or the S.H.A.P.E. Test. Both are available online.

CHAPTER 13

MORE TIPS FOR THE TEMPEST

"Often, we seek advice from people who are stuck in the same boat that we are in."

READING TIME

As you read Chapter 13: "More Tips for the Tempest" in *Standing Strong in the Storm*, reflect on the questions and scriptures.

REFLECT AND TAKE ACTION:

In your own words, what is wisdom? Where do you go to get more of it?

_____
_____
_____
_____
_____
_____

What do you think is the best way to prepare for a coming storm? How do you fortify your life and beliefs, knowing a storm may be looming on the horizon?

_____
_____
_____
_____
_____
_____

What are your main priorities? What do you think God wants you to prioritize more or less?

_____
_____
_____
_____
_____
_____

> *If any of you lacks wisdom, you should ask God, who gives generously to all without finding fault, and it will be given to you.*
>
> —James 1:5

Consider the scripture above and answer the following questions:

In what areas of your life do you lack wisdom? Have you ever thought of asking God to supply you with wisdom? What has been His response?

_____
_____
_____
_____
_____

Why is the state of a person's heart important when they ask God to grant them wisdom?

_____
_____
_____
_____
_____

What is your routine for seeking godly wisdom? How can you acquire more godly wisdom by altering your daily habits?

_____
_____
_____
_____
_____

How do you stay anchored to God and the truth? What steps do you take to ensure you don't wash away in a tumultuous storm?

_____
_____
_____
_____

Why do you think preparing before the storm strikes is so important? What happens if we wait?

_____
_____
_____
_____

What do you think the Lord wants you to cast overboard in order to reorder your priorities, lighten your load, and make it through the storm?

_____
_____
_____
_____

CHAPTER 14

THE OTHER SIDE: WHEN YOU HAVE CROSSED OVER

"An untold story makes no impact."

READING TIME

As you read Chapter 14: "The Other Side: When You Have Crossed Over" in *Standing Strong in the Storm*, reflect on the questions and scriptures.

REFLECT AND TAKE ACTION:

Are there any stories in your life of God's deliverance that you haven't shared with others? What's stopping you?

_____
_____
_____
_____
_____
_____
_____
_____
_____
_____

Can you think of someone else's testimony that has positively impacted you? What if they had never told it?

_____
_____
_____
_____
_____
_____
_____
_____
_____
_____

> *". . . But you will receive power when the Holy Spirit comes on you; and you will be my witnesses in Jerusalem, and in Judea and Samaria, and to the ends of the earth."*
>
> —Acts 1:8

Consider the scripture above and answer the following questions:

What kind of power is Jesus speaking of here?

_____
_____
_____

How are you a witness for Jesus Christ?

_____
_____
_____

What situation in your life has He helped you through that allows you to be a more effective witness for Him?

_____
_____
_____
_____

Have you ever been confused about which path to take? How did you discover which way to go?

_____
_____
_____
_____

What principles discussed in this chapter do you need to apply to your life to be a more effective witness for God?

_____
_____
_____

Do the desires of your heart line up with God's Word and His calling for your life? How can you tell?

_____
_____
_____

What is your God-given dream?

_____
_____
_____

What are three takeaways from *Standing Strong in the Storm* and this study guide that you can start applying to your routine, thoughts, and focus today?

1. _____
_____

2. _____
_____

3. _____
_____

www.ingramcontent.com/pod-product-compliance
Lightning Source LLC
Chambersburg PA
CBHW062123080426
42734CB00012B/2962